Meet the MIXELS™

Written by Shari Last

LONDON, NEW YORK, MUNICH,
MELBOURNE AND DELHI

Editor Shari Last
Designer Rhys Thomas
Pre-Production Producer Marc Staples
Producer Louise Minihane
Managing Editor Elizabeth Dowsett
Design Manager Ron Stobbart
Publishing Manager Julie Ferris
Art Director Lisa Lanzarini
Publishing Director Simon Beecroft

Designed for DK by
Sandra Perry

Reading Consultant
Maureen Fernandes

First published in in Great Britain in 2014 by
Dorling Kindersley Limited
80 Strand, London, WC2R 0RL
A Penguin Random House Company

10 9 8 7 6 5 4 3 2 1
001—255728—Sep/2014

Colour reproduction by Alta Image, UK
Printed and bound in China by South China

Discover more at
www.dk.com
www.LEGO.com

Contents

4   The Mixels™

6   Flain

8   Vulk and Zorch

10   The Infernites' Guide to Fire Safety

12   Krader, Seismo and Shuff

14   Shuff's Maze

16   Teslo, Zaptor and Volectro

18   Flurr, Lunk and Slumbo

20   Breaking News: Slumbo Wakes Up!

22   Scorpi, Footi and Hoogi

24   Jawg, Gobba and Chomly

26   Fang Gang Menu

28   Kraw, Tentro and Balk

30   Flexercise

32   Glomp, Glurt and Torts

34   Mixels Mix

36   Magnifo, Mesmo and Wizwuz

38   Many Mixels

40   Let's Party!

42   Quiz

44   Glossary

45   Index

46   Guide for Parents

The Mixels™

What are these strange creatures?
They are Mixels!

Mixels are colourful, funny
and always ready for adventure.

Let's meet the Mixels
and join in the fun.

Flain

Flain is a fiery Infernite.
He is so clever that his brain
sometimes bursts into flames!

The Infernites live in
a place full of hot lava
and rivers of fire.

Who else lives here?

Vulk and Zorch

Vulk has scorching hot hands,
so watch out for his high fives!

Zorch is a cheeky Infernite. He speeds along, leaving fire trailing behind him.

THE INFERNITES'
Guide to Fire Safety

1. Never stand behind Zorch.

2. Wear gloves before giving Vulk a high five.

3. When Flain starts thinking, run away.

4. Never go swimming in the rivers of fire.

5. Keep a fire extinguisher nearby, just in case.

Krader, Seismo and Shuff

The hard-working Cragsters spend their time digging underground tunnels.

Krader has a wrecking ball fist.

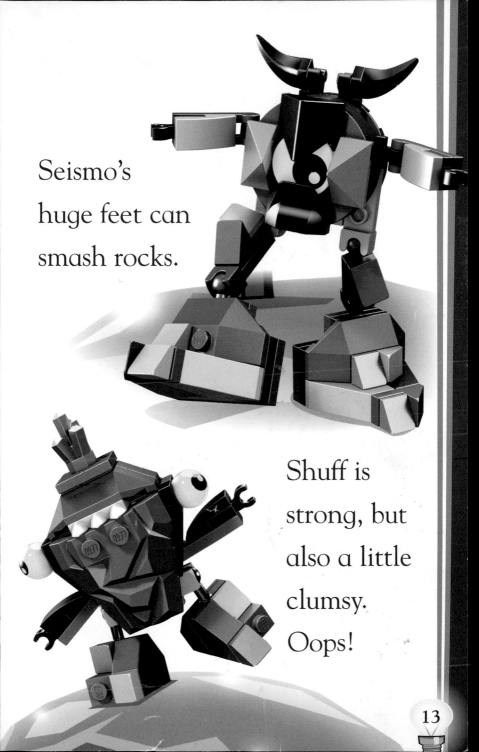

Seismo's huge feet can smash rocks.

Shuff is strong, but also a little clumsy. Oops!

13

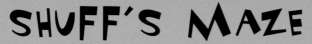

SHUFF'S MAZE

Oh dear! Shuff is lost in his own underground tunnel. He was working so hard that now he can't remember the way out. Can you help him find the way back to his friends?

Teslo, Zaptor and Volectro

Who are these crazy Mixels?

They are Teslo, Zaptor and Volectro.

These yellow Electroids
are full of sizzling energy.
They live high in the mountains,
where they catch lightning.

Flurr, Lunk and Slumbo

Brrr. It is cold here.

Let's meet the Frosticons

who live in frozen volcanoes.

This is Flurr.

This is Lunk.

Can you spot Slumbo?
Slumbo is very, very relaxed.
He is nearly always asleep.

LEGO® MIXELS™ NEWS

BREAKING NEWS:
Slumbo Wakes Up!

Every Mixel was surprised yesterday when Slumbo, the famously sleepy Frosticon, woke up all by himself!

It is unusual for Slumbo to stir from his slumber on his own.

It usually takes four or more Mixels to wake him up.

Slumbo's friend Flurr cannot explain it. "Last time I looked, he was fast asleep. Now he's awake.

Awake at last! Slumbo surprises everyone.

I just don't understand it!"

Another Frosticon, Lunk, has an idea: "Slumbo must be excited because we are going to build an ice tower today. Slumbo loves building with ice."

Perhaps it is because Slumbo loves building ice towers.

The only question is, does he like building ice towers more than he likes sleeping?

What do you think?

Scorpi, Footi and Hoogi

Hello Spikels!

Scorpi loves pillow fights, but beware his prickly tail!

Footi cannot
sit still.
His spiky feet
are always
moving.

Hoogi always
wants to cuddle,
but his claws
sometimes get
in the way.

Jawg, Gobba and Chomly

The Fang Gang are always hungry. Jawg has huge teeth for fast chewing.

Gobba's tongue can find the best food around.

24

Chomly will eat... ANYTHING!
His bad breath keeps everyone
else away.

Fang Gang Menu

What we have eaten today:

1 coconapple
(this delicious fruit is
half a coconut, half an apple!)

2 bicycle wheels

2 sandwiches

8 cookironis
(a tasty mix between a cookie
and a piece of macaroni!)

Chomly

3 ice creams

Jawg

1 ant

1 pea

1 dustbin lid

6 cupcakes

6 toy cupcakes

lots of grass

and a bit of mud

YUM!
What a feast!

Gobba

Kraw, Tentro and Balk

Welcome to the Rubberlands. Can you find the funny Flexers who live here?

Kraw loves bouncing up and down.

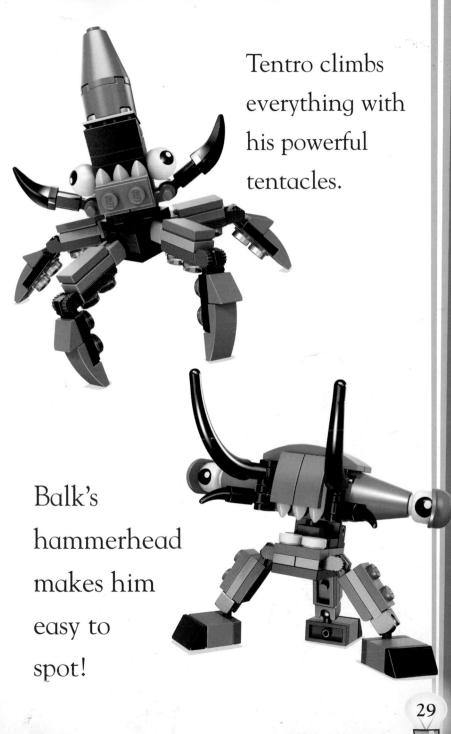

Tentro climbs everything with his powerful tentacles.

Balk's hammerhead makes him easy to spot!

FLEXERCISE

Keeping fit is important.
Follow these easy flexercises to stay
healthy and have lots of fun!

1. JUMP

Jump up and down. If you are very bouncy,
make sure you don't bump your head!

2.CLIMB

Climb things. Make sure you are safe and do not climb too high. If you have tentacles, you could try climbing upside down.

3.WIGGLE

Wiggle your head, arms, legs and body. Shake your fingers and toes. If you have a head shaped like a hammer, try not to hit it against walls and other things.

Glomp, Glurt and Torts

The gooey Glorp Corp live in the swamps.

Glomp plays games, even though he has a runny nose.

Glurt
dribbles when
he is happy.

Torts is messy.
His slimy hands make
everything sticky.

Mixels Mix

Sometimes, Mixels like to
mix up their own pieces
with their friends' pieces.
They become completely
new creatures!
Look what happens
when two Mixels mix.

Krader   +   Zaptor

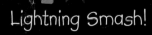

Lightning Smash!

Gobba + Kraw = Hungry Tentacles!

Glurt + Footi = Slimy Stomp!

Magnifo, Mesmo and Wizwuz

Introducing the Wiztastics!
These magicians love to
put on a show.

Magnifo wants
his magic to
be amazing.

Mesmo is his shy assistant.

Wizwuz loves performing,
even if he sometimes
makes mistakes.

Many Mixels

Now you have met the Mixels.
They are all very different.
Which ones are the funniest?
Which are the strongest?
This chart will help you decide.

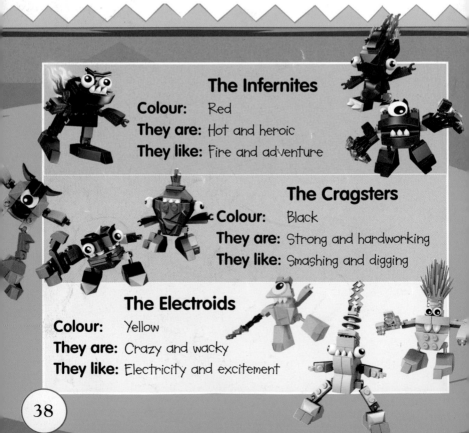

The Infernites
Colour: Red
They are: Hot and heroic
They like: Fire and adventure

The Cragsters
Colour: Black
They are: Strong and hardworking
They like: Smashing and digging

The Electroids
Colour: Yellow
They are: Crazy and wacky
They like: Electricity and excitement

The Frosticons

Colour: Blue
They are: Relaxed and cool
They like: Ice, snow and everything cold!

The Spikels

Colour: Beige
They are: Playful and happy
They like: Hugs and having lots of fun

The Fang Gang

Colour: Brown
They are: Hungry, hungry, hungry
They like: Whatever they can eat

The Flexers

Colour: Orange
They are: Bendy and funny
They like: Moving and bouncing

The Glorp Corp

Colour: Green
They are: Gooey and goofy
They like: Playing games with friends

The Wiztastics

Colour: Purple
They are: Magicians
They like: Doing magic tricks and
amazing their friends

39

Let's Party!

Now that you have met
the Mixels, it is time to
play. Bring some food,
a pot of goo, a magic
wand, a cosy pillow
and a fire extinguisher.

   Let's have some fun!

Mix Festival

Quiz

1. Which Mixels live in a place full of hot lava?

2. Which Cragster has a wrecking ball fist?

3. Which Mixels are yellow?

4. Which Mixel is nearly always asleep?

5. Who loves pillow fights?

6. Who has bad breath?

7. Where do
the Flexers live?

8. What does Kraw love doing?

9. Whose hands
make everything
sticky?

10. What colour
are the Wiztastics?

Answers on page 45

Glossary

assistant
a person who helps someone else

coconapple
a fruit that is half a coconut, half an apple

cookironi
a snack that is half a cookie, half macaroni

fiery
something made of fire or flames

fire extinguisher
a machine that puts out fires

lava
hot, melted rock that flows overground

magician
a person who performs magic

scorching
extremely hot

slumber
a light sleep

tentacles
a flexible part of the body that is used to touch or climb things

volcanoes
mountains that sometimes shoot lava from the top

wrecking ball
a big, heavy ball that knocks things down

Index

Cragsters 12, 38

Electroids 17, 38

Fang Gang 24, 26, 39

fire 6, 9–11, 38, 41

Flexers 28, 30, 39

friends 14, 20, 34, 39

Frosticons 18, 20–21, 39

Glorp Corp 32, 39

Infernites 6, 9–10, 38

Spikels 22, 39

Wiztastics 36, 39

Answers to the quiz on pages 42 and 43:
1. The Infernites 2. Krader 3. The Electroids
4. Slumbo 5. Scorpi 6. Chomly
7. The Rubberlands 8. Bouncing 9. Torts 10. Purple

Guide for Parents

DK Reads is a three-level reading series for children, developing the habit of reading widely for both pleasure and information. These books have exciting running text interspersed with a range of reading genres to suit your child's reading ability, as required by the school curriculum. Each book is designed to develop your child's reading skills, fluency, grammar awareness and comprehension in order to build confidence and engagement when reading.

Ready for a *Beginning to Read* book
YOUR CHILD SHOULD

- be using phonics, including combinations of consonants, such as bl, gl and sm, to read unfamiliar words; and common word endings, such as plurals, ing, ed and ly.
- be using the storyline, illustrations and the grammar of a sentence to check and correct their own reading.
- be pausing briefly at commas, and for longer at full stops; and altering his/her expression to respond to question, exclamation and speech marks.

A Valuable And Shared Reading Experience

For many children, reading requires much effort but adult participation can make this both fun and easier. So here are a few tips on how to use this book with your child.

TIP 1: Check out the contents together before your child begins:

- Read the text about the book on the back cover.
- Read through and discuss the contents page together to heighten your child's interest and expectation.
- Briefly discuss any unfamiliar or difficult words on the contents page.

- Chat about the non-fiction reading features used in the book, such as headings, captions, recipes, lists or charts.

This introduction helps to put your child in control and makes the reading challenge less daunting.

TIP 2: Support your child as he/she reads the story pages:

- Give the book to your child to read and turn the pages.
- Where necessary, encourage your child to break a word into syllables, sound out each one and then flow the syllables together. Ask him/her to reread the sentence to check the meaning.
- When there's a question mark or an exclamation mark, encourage your child to vary his/her voice as he/she reads the sentence. Demonstrate how to do this if it is helpful.

TIP 3: Praise, share and chat:

- The factual pages tend to be more difficult than the story pages, and are designed to be shared with your child.
- Ask questions about the text and the meaning of the words used. Ask your child to suggest his/her own quiz questions. These help to develop comprehension skills and awareness of the language used.

A FEW ADDITIONAL TIPS

- Try and read together everyday. Little and often is best. After 10 minutes, only keep going if your child wants to read on.
- Always encourage your child to have a go at reading difficult words by themselves. Praise any self-corrections, for example, "I like the way you sounded out that word and then changed the way you said it, to make sense".
- Read other books of different types to your child just for enjoyment and information.

Here are some other DK Reads you might enjoy.

Beginning to Read

LEGO® Legends of Chima™: Tribes of Chima
Enter the mysterious land of Chima and discover
the amazing animal tribes who live there.

LEGO® Friends: Perfect Pets
Learn all about Mia, Olivia, Andrea, Stephanie and Emma's
pets – and discover how much fun pets can be!

Star Wars Rebels™: Meet the Rebels
Meet the *Star Wars Rebels* heroes and learn all about the
enemies from the evil Empire they are rebelling against.

Starting to Read Alone

LEGO® Legends of Chima™: Heroes' Quest
Who are the mysterious Legend Beasts? Join the heroes of Chima
on their quest to find these mythical creatures.

LEGO® Friends: Summer Adventures
Enjoy a summer of fun in Heartlake City with Emma,
Mia, Andrea, Stephanie, Olivia and friends.

Star Wars™: What Makes a Monster?
Meet some of the most fearsome monsters in the *Star Wars* galaxy.
Discover brutal beasts, scary hunters and strange creatures.